Begin Again

Julia A. Royston

Edited by: Claude R. Royston

BK Royston Publishing
Jeffersonville, IN

BK Royston Publishing
P. O. Box 4321
Jeffersonville, IN 47131
502-802-5385
http://www.bkroystonpublishing.com
bkroystonpublishing@gmail.com

© Copyright – 2016

Cover Design: Bill Lacy

ISBN-13: 978-0692666043

Printed in the United States of America

Dedication

I dedicate this book to anyone who has ever
had something happen in your life that made
you start all over again. Know that you may
be delayed but destiny still is front of you and
you will get there. God's promises are true
and absolute.

Just Begin Again...

Acknowledgements

First, I acknowledge my Lord and Savior Jesus Christ for giving me all of my gifts and especially my gift to write His words.

My husband who is always supportive, loving and encouraging me to utilize all of my gifts and talents. Thank you honey.

To my mother, Dr. Daisy Foree, who is my number one cheerleader and always tells me, "hang in there, you can do it." To my father, Dr. Jack Foree, who is never far away from me in spirit or my heart. I only have to look in the mirror each day to see him.

To Rev. Claude and Mrs. Lillie Royston who support me in everything I do. Especially, Rev. Royston for his careful eye to detail and his sensitive heart to content.

To the rest of my family, I love you and thank you for your prayers, support and love.

Introduction

I have been a teacher for twenty years at the printing of this book. I have been singing for more than forty years. I have begun to coach and speak at workshops and conferences for the past ten years. I use my voice a lot. I am called to teach. I was prayed for and confirmed about this teaching call on my life. For more than twenty years, my thyroid has been growing tumors surrounding the thing that I was to use the most, my vocal chords. It is a hereditary condition that my father had and his mother before him. In February of 2015, I had major surgery to remove a much enlarged thyroid which had grown to more than six inches inside my body. It took two surgeries in the same night because a blood vessel burst and they had to go back in and stop the bleeding. After that surgery, I have not been able to talk, sing or teach the same. I had to start all over again. I had to re-record music, lower the keys musically and "Begin Again" using my voice in a whole new way. My speaking voice is lower, my singing voice is different and as a result I have to prepare differently to sing and speak. I am grateful and thankful that I am able to still perform musically and continue my career as a teacher. There are times when I have questioned God about it. I wondered why He didn't miraculously heal me. He could have but He didn't. I wondered why He gave me new music that I have to struggle to sing with a voice that doesn't have the stamina as before. In times past, I could sing clearly out of my sleep but now I have to warm up, rehearse, practice and clear my voice before I sing. Then I must use a warm down process even after I sing. It is different. Forty plus years of doing something with ease one way and now I must learn to operate a different way. I must "Begin Again." No matter what situation is going on in your life right now, say yes, go through the process, fine tune it or get a 'new normal' and "Begin Again."

For me, God said, "I want to get the Glory and Honor from your voice this time at its weakest. This time, it is ALL about my anointing and not about your gift."

Beginning Again, Julia

Action Plan

Vision Board Parties, Meetings, Luncheons and workshops have recently been all the rage especially at the beginning of a new year. I think that all of these events are great, but having a vision and putting that vision into action are two different things. I have seen vision boards collect dust and nothing on the board come to fruition. More than a vision board or vision plans or vision goals you need to have an action plan. What are you going to do to make your vision come to pass? When are you going to have that action step done and completed? Set a date. Even if it is not exact, set a target date. When you have something that you are shooting for or aiming at, there is motivation, drive and a great chance for effort to be put forth to make that goal come true.

Julia Royston

_____

_____

_____

_____

_____

_____

_____

_____

_____

_____

_____

_____

_____

_____

_____

_____

_____

_____

_____

Begin Again

You've tried once. Whatever that thing you wanted to do. It may not have worked before but try it again. Begin all over again. If it is something that you have always wanted to do, longed to do and good at doing, you can do it. Don't give up but Begin Again. Things happen. Life has its ups and downs and things get in the way of your success. But, if you really want it bad enough, you should be willing to "Begin Again."

Julia Royston

_____

_____

_____

_____

_____

_____

_____

_____

_____

_____

_____

_____

_____

_____

_____

_____

_____

_____

_____

_____

_____

Bury it and Let it Go

You know why the coroner has a job? It's to handle dead people in the world. Dead people were not designed to remain among the living. The dead thing will kill the living thing, physically and emotionally. This is the reason why when someone dies, we call the police, the coroner and the funeral home. These organizations and industries know what to do with the dead. To begin again, you may have to call an outside police, coroner and funeral home to help you remove these people, places or things but do it. It's killing you to keep that dead thing around. You can't move forward with it sleeping, eating and playing games in your mind every day. Ask for help. Get a doctor. You may not die physically but your spirit, drive or ambition will die with that dead thing. Finally, after you bury it, be sure to let it go and don't dig it back up.

Julia Royston

_____

_____

_____

_____

_____

_____

_____

_____

_____

_____

_____

_____

_____

_____

_____

_____

_____

_____

_____

Celebrate Your Progress

Celebrations are always fun whether it is a large gathering in a stadium, at a restaurant with friends or home alone with a cup of hot chocolate and a movie. Take some time out and enjoy the moment. Enjoy your team. Enjoy the accomplishment. Just celebrate. You have worked hard. You struggled and came out victorious. Do something fun. Get a massage. Do nothing and rest but above all be happy and celebrate.

_____

_____

_____

_____

_____

_____

_____

_____

_____

_____

_____

_____

_____

_____

_____

_____

_____

_____

_____

_____

_____

Begin Again

Change.Me

At my job, to begin the process to change the password for access to a computer, I must begin with change.me and then a new id or password comes next. This idea of change.me has stuck with me for more than a year now. I believe that God was telling me that it was time to change some things within and around me before other things would change in my life. So, I ask you today to ask yourself the hard question of what do I need to change about me? We sometimes want others to change but the only person that we can really control is ourselves. So, in your quiet time, devotion time or meditation time, ask yourself, what do I need to change.me?

9

Julia Royston

_____

_____

_____

_____

_____

_____

_____

_____

_____

_____

_____

_____

_____

_____

_____

_____

_____

_____

_____

_____

_____

Decisions

Sometimes even when you don't want to
decide, you have made a decision.
When you do nothing, you have made a
decision. Decide carefully. Your
decisions can affect not only you, your
life but the lives of others around you.
Get all of the information you can to
make the best decision possible.
Finally, when you come to a conclusion
and actually decide, stick to it. Don't
waiver. You may be scared but face
that fear with the knowledge in your
heart that you did the right thing. Don't
live in regret but decide to live in your
truth. Make wise decisions. A great
decision today will make a fabulous life
tomorrow.

Julia Royston

_____

_____

_____

_____

_____

_____

_____

_____

_____

_____

_____

_____

_____

_____

_____

_____

_____

_____

Begin Again

Don't Discount

Who doesn't love a sale? I do. Get me
to a clearance, going out of business or
just reduced prices sale and I can
always find something to purchase.
Why? Because I don't like to pay the
high price of some items. It's not worth
it. I'll just wait until it goes on sale or
better yet, clearance or close out. Some
of your reading this have put your life on
sale, clearance or auction to the highest
bidder. You make it convenient,
reasonable and affordable to be with
you and in your circle of influence. The
price is so right that anyone, any day
can pay the price. The person doesn't
have to learn about you or study you or
put something in layaway or even
endure a 90 day problem. You're on
sale. Buy here, pay here. That may be
the reason why you have so much
drama and trouble in your life. Don't
charge the regular price but charge

couture prices, out of the reach of the average person. Make the price for access into your life, selective and exclusive. You are too valuable. Act like it and no matter what, don't discount

Begin Again

_____

_____

_____

_____

_____

_____

_____

_____

_____

_____

_____

_____

_____

_____

_____

_____

_____

_____

_____

_____

_____

_____

Julia Royston

_____

_____

_____

_____

_____

_____

_____

_____

_____

_____

_____

_____

_____

_____

_____

_____

_____

_____

_____

_____

Fight for Your Life

When you have had major trouble in your life and you begin to see a way out of it, be willing to fight for the life that you want to have. You have been given a second, third or one hundredth chance to live. Take it. Do what is necessary to live your best life. Fight for it! Let nothing or no one stop you from having the life that you've always wanted. There are some things in life that are so precious that you should be willing to literally fight for to have. I can encourage you but I can't fight for your life for you. You have to do it. You have to want it. You have to fight for it. I am fighting for the life I want. What about you?

Julia Royston

_____

_____

_____

_____

_____

_____

_____

_____

_____

_____

_____

_____

_____

_____

_____

_____

_____

_____

Begin Again

Fix It

Neither my husband nor I like for things to be around us that don't work. I am a regular at Goodwill because I will put what's broken or what we don't want in a black bag and drop it off in a quick minute. If it can't fixed, I don't want it. I don't like things laying around that don't work. If it works, I'll use it. If I don't want to use it any more, I give it away. But, first, I try to fix it. What needs to be fixed before you begin again? What have you been holding onto that's broken? Fix it. Plain and simple fix it. Don't love on it. Don't make excuses for it. Don't pretend it works when it doesn't, just fix it. If you can't fix it alone, get a professional who specializes and a track record for fixing what's broken in your house, life or emotions. Fix it. That small thing that needs fixing will turn into a huge thing if you don't fix it right now. Just one more time, fix it.

Begin Again

_____

_____

_____

_____

_____

_____

_____

_____

_____

_____

_____

_____

_____

_____

_____

_____

_____

_____

_____

_____

_____

Julia Royston

_____

_____

_____

_____

_____

_____

_____

_____

_____

_____

_____

_____

_____

_____

_____

_____

_____

_____

_____

_____

Focus

Begin again by gathering more information to really focusing on your goals and dreams. When you are focused you ask more questions and find out from the experienced experts. When you are focused you read everything related to what you are about to do. Why? What you are focused on could literally transform your life and you don't want to waste any more time than necessary. You may have been distracted in the past and looking back, realize that you didn't arrive at the desired destination or reach the goals that you desired. This time maintain your focus, remove any and every distraction and zero in on your target and don't stop until you reach your destination. Go ahead and Focus.

Julia Royston

_____

_____

_____

_____

_____

_____

_____

_____

_____

_____

_____

_____

_____

_____

_____

_____

_____

_____

_____

Forgive

Forgiveness is a hard subject to tackle and an even harder act to carry out. Some people hurt you so badly that you don't want to forgive them. Why? Because forgiveness is a gift. Forgiveness is one of those tasks that takes you outside of yourself and requires God to do it. Forgiveness should not be taken lightly just because the words, 'I forgive you," are few. For some, forgiveness is given through pain, agony and hurt. Forgiveness does not negate the act or words that need to be forgiven, it just puts a limit, stopping place and end to the reliving it over and over again. Forgiveness does not mean that the person who hurt you is immediately restored to their initial place of trust and access to your life. Trust must be earned and re-established. As someone who has had to forgive someone who hurt me deeply, the

Julia Royston

unforgiveness was sowing a seed of bitterness, anger and strife in my heart. This seed was going to be a weed that would kill the flow of good that was to reside in my heart if I didn't forgive and kill the unforgiveness at the root.

Begin Again

_____

_____

_____

_____

_____

_____

_____

_____

_____

_____

_____

_____

_____

_____

_____

_____

_____

_____

_____

_____

Julia Royston

_____

_____

_____

_____

_____

_____

_____

_____

_____

_____

_____

_____

_____

_____

_____

_____

_____

_____

_____

_____

_____

_____

Is There Not a Cause?

When you begin again there should be a reason, good or bad. It doesn't matter whether a tragedy occurred or things weren't going right, just begin again. Starting again will have even more meaning when there is a reason, cause or origin for the effort. When you have a goal in mind or person that you are working for or a heartfelt reason, it makes it all worthwhile. Everyone doesn't have to agree on your reason or even approve but deep inside, you know and it is right for you so that's all that matters. What is your cause? What is driving you to change? What is making you want to start over? That's your cause. That's your reason. That's all that matters.

Julia Royston

_____

_____

_____

_____

_____

_____

_____

_____

_____

_____

_____

_____

_____

_____

_____

_____

_____

_____

Begin Again

Love Yourself

When you are starting all over again, you have to begin with you. It's not about your friends, your family or neighbors but you. What does God want with you? What is His plan for your life? Until you can find out what He wants from you, you can't get help from others or even know who you need to have in your life period. Start by loving yourself enough to find out. Let others know that I'm too busy working on me to be working on you. I love myself too much to stay mediocre or average. I must become the best self that God intended. If that means not being in your company, so be it. If that means walking alone for a period, so be it. If that means changing my name, so be it. If that means changing my address, so be it. Love yourself first. When you love yourself, you won't tolerate certain things that don't please you, give Glory

31

to God and don't move you toward your purpose. How much do you really love yourself?

Begin Again

_____

_____

_____

_____

_____

_____

_____

_____

_____

_____

_____

_____

_____

_____

_____

_____

_____

_____

_____

Julia Royston

_____

_____

_____

_____

_____

_____

_____

_____

_____

_____

_____

_____

_____

_____

_____

_____

_____

_____

_____

_____

_____

Mistakes Rather than Regret

Neither mistakes nor regret sound good when striving to live the abundant life. So, I have decided to make mistakes rather than do nothing and live in regret land. I have decided to make the best educated decision that I can, count up the cost, pray as well as ask for help and then go for it. I am only going to live once on this side of the grave. I also know that I will learn a great deal from my mistakes and hopefully, won't make those same exact mistakes again. There will be other mistakes made but the ones from my past, I will strive to not make again. Mistakes vs. Regret? Regrets are too difficult to live with. I'll take mistakes. At least with a mistake, I was doing something rather than nothing.

Julia Royston

_____

_____

_____

_____

_____

_____

_____

_____

_____

_____

_____

_____

_____

_____

_____

_____

_____

_____

Begin Again

Practice Doesn't Make Perfect

Practice doesn't always make you perfect. Ask the Olympic athlete who practices and works for four years to compete in the Olympics. Are they perfect? Some are but others are just the best that one time on that one day and they are a champion for a lifetime. Practice makes you experienced. Each and every experience that we have in life should make us knowledgeable, better decision makers and a witness to what we do and do not want for our lives. Practice makes you better. Practice makes you good, great and a teacher for the inexperienced. Perfection is too high a standard.

Julia Royston

_____

_____

_____

_____

_____

_____

_____

_____

_____

_____

_____

_____

_____

_____

_____

_____

_____

_____

_____

_____

Rebuilt Trust

One of the hardest things to do when you are beginning again is to trust. You trusted before and you were hurt, disappointed or lied to. When you begin again, you have to move slower, be more careful and ask more questions to rebuild the trust. Trust wasn't broken overnight and it won't be rebuilt overnight either. On the other hand, for you to go higher, do more and go further, you will have to learn to trust someone, sometime and with something.

You are not an island. You cannot do it all yourself. You tried it once before and you ended up exhausted, frustrated and burnt out. Furthermore, there wasn't much accomplished because you were trying to do it all alone. This time let trust build step by step and moment by moment. When trust has been broken

Julia Royston

even this time, don't lose heart in all
people but be careful with that one
person.

Begin Again

_____

_____

_____

_____

_____

_____

_____

_____

_____

_____

_____

_____

_____

_____

_____

_____

_____

_____

_____

_____

Julia Royston

_____

_____

_____

_____

_____

_____

_____

_____

_____

_____

_____

_____

_____

_____

_____

_____

_____

_____

_____

Begin Again

Transformation

I love the action movies *"Transformers."*
It was incredible all of the stunts,
actions, sequences and cars used in
those movies. The old cartoon song,
"transformers more than meets the eye"
always comes to mind. Have you ever
been overlooked or ignored because
people couldn't see the real you? There
was more to you inside that you were
displaying or allowed to display on the
outside. It's time to transform into the
new you. Transform yourself into the
you that you were always meant to be
down inside. Transform from what you
have allowed people to see into the
person that you want people to see.
The real you. God sees it and knew it
before you were born. You have to
embrace the process of transformation
and then fly.

_____

_____

_____

_____

_____

_____

_____

_____

_____

_____

_____

_____

_____

_____

_____

_____

_____

_____

_____

_____

_____

Begin Again

What's the Destination?

I love to travel and explore new places, new cities and foods. My husband is equally as adventurous which is wonderful. I hate getting lost so we have wonderful phones complete with a GPS/Maps systems to guide us to the destination whether we are in a new city or there is a new place to visit in our home town. Where are you headed? As you begin this new life's journey, where do you want to arrive? What's your ideal location to somewhere land? It may not be a new location physically but could be a new location in your mind. A new mindset takes as much effort as packing your clothes and boarding a plane. You have a destination in your mind and you must have a daily plan. Prepare and pray that you arrive safely. What's the destination? Will you know it once you get there? Will the sand be as white or the water just as blue? Will you be able to sleep better at night? Pay all of your bills in the same month? Launch that business or finally finish that book. Whatever or where ever it is, get there. I've got somewhere to go. What's your destination?

Begin Again

_____

_____

_____

_____

_____

_____

_____

_____

_____

_____

_____

_____

_____

_____

_____

_____

_____

_____

_____

_____

Julia Royston

_____

_____

_____

_____

_____

_____

_____

_____

_____

_____

_____

_____

_____

_____

_____

_____

_____

_____

_____

Begin Again

Where Art Thou?

You have to start where you are. Where are you now? What is your current status? How much money do you have right now? How much money do you need to move forward right now? Who can you rely on right now in your life? The past is the past. The future is so far off you don't have a clue. All you know is the now, the present and the current of a situation. Start there and don't live in the regret of the past and the fear of the future. Start right here. Admit it to yourself exactly where you are right now. You can't be true to yourself until you do. If someone wanted to help you, you would have to be able to verbalize exactly where you are now. Tell the truth. Be honest with them and yourself. The truth hurts but you won't be able to move forward from here until you do. Take a deep breath. Wipe the tears and answer the question, where art thou?

Julia Royston

_____

_____

_____

_____

_____

_____

_____

_____

_____

_____

_____

_____

_____

_____

_____

_____

_____

_____

_____

_____

Yield Don't Stop

The yield sign is designed to keep traffic moving especially when two lanes of traffic are merging into one. The objective is for one lane of cars to yield when other cars are coming. If there are no cars coming in the non-yield lane, the cars in the yield move freely at the speed limit without stopping. I recently have to travel in one of these intersections with a yield lane and a non-yield lane. People stop at the yield sign even if no cars are coming. It makes me develop road rage. I yell at the other driver as though he can hear me. Of course he can't, but it makes me feel better. I digress. But do you know that there are people in this world stopping their life for someone else? There may be cause for yield. A child that is sick will slow you down. An accident that produces a bill and delays some of your plans will bring reason to pause, think and regroup but, should you stop? No way. Keep moving forward. It may take a little longer but yield don't stop.

Begin Again

_____

_____

_____

_____

_____

_____

_____

_____

_____

_____

_____

_____

_____

_____

_____

_____

_____

_____

_____

_____

Julia Royston

_____

_____

_____

_____

_____

_____

_____

_____

_____

_____

_____

_____

_____

_____

_____

_____

_____

_____

_____

_____

Begin Again

You are a Gift

I love to receive and give gifts. People who love to give can be some of the best gift givers ever because they actually think about the person that they are giving the gift to. Now, giving gifts can be a tricky business. What if the person doesn't like the gift after they open it? What if the person never uses the gift and throws it in the trash. I give gift cards because they are the perfect gift and it always fits. I confess that I don't have to think that hard with a gift card. God loves to give gifts as well. He gave you as a gift to the earth. Some people may not receive you as a gift or discover the gift that is you, but you are a gift just the same. Embrace the gifting, talents and abilities that you have but more importantly, embrace you as the gift that you are to the world.

Julia Royston

_____
_____
_____
_____
_____
_____
_____
_____
_____
_____
_____
_____
_____
_____
_____
_____
_____
_____
_____

About the Author

Julia Royston is an author, publishing and motivational speaker born and raised in Louisville, KY. Julia is the oldest of 3 daughters in a Christian family and is married to Mr. Brian K. Royston. Julia earned a B.A. in Accounting, two Masters Degrees in Information Science and a doctorate in Religious Education from Bellarmine University, University of Kentucky, Spalding University and Grace Bible College, Niles, OH, respectively. Julia is a public elementary school Computer Technology Teacher/Media Specialist by profession.

Julia has appeared on The Bobby Jones Presents New Artist Showcase and ministered with notables such as Dr. Jackie McCullough, Pastor Donnie McClurkin, Bishop Noel Jones, Bishop

Julia Royston

Tudor Bismarck, Myron Williams and Bishop Richard "Mr. Clean" White. In December 2004 and 2005, Julia toured Switzerland with the Voices of Gospel Concert Series.

Julia has been singing since nine years of age and to date has recorded several music projects including, "Joy in His Presence", "A New Season in Word and Song", "Hymns for Him", "For Your Glory Lord" and in the Fall of 2016 is set to release her next full project, "Begin Again."

In 2002, Julia established For the Kingdom Ministries with the mission to "Build God's People to Build the Kingdom of God" through education, empowerment and encouragement through inspirational music, high quality materials and messages of hope.

Begin Again

In 2011, BK Royston Publishing Company was established and released its first book titled, "How Hot is Your Love Life? Return to Your first Love." To date Julia Royston has published 20 books with BK Royston Publishing Company, LLC and has signed 30 authors to her company and published more than 60 books. For more information about BK Royston Publishing, click here and visithttp://bkroystonpublishing.com.

Julia Royston Enterprises LLC was established in 2013 to assist people to walk in their purpose through transformational virtual, group and individual coaching. Visit: http://www.juliaroystonenterprises.com to learn more about and sign up for the many coaching programs offered by Julia Royston Enterprises.

Julia Royston

In 2015, a second publishing company, Royal Media Publishing was established to provide an outlet for the authors with mainstream topics that need to be addressed and brought to the forefront for a global audience.

Currently, Julia Royston hosts a daily motivational Periscope called Julia Royston, the "Message Motivator", and "When Authors Meet" workshops for authors around the country and retreats, conferences and masterminds for business owners as well as authors.

The year 2016 marks 5 years that BK Royston Publishing has been in business. Julia Royston continues to travel the country speaking, singing, empowering and inspiring people around the world to write, publish their books and to live the abundant life that is their Purpose and Destiny.

Begin Again

Keep up with Julia on Social Media by following or liking her pages on Facebook, Twitter, LinkedIn, Instagram, Periscope and Blab.